A Woman's World

A Woman's World

GRACE PATTERSON

Illustrated by Marissa Patterson

RESOURCE *Publications* · Eugene, Oregon

A WOMAN'S WORLD

Resource Publications
An Imprint of Wipf and Stock Publishers
199 W. 8th Ave., Suite 3
Eugene, OR 97401

www.wipfandstock.com

PAPERBACK ISBN: 978-1-6667-6379-9
HARDCOVER ISBN: 978-1-6667-6380-5
EBOOK ISBN: 978-1-6667-6381-2

01/19/23

Just nineteen
Naive, young, and free
Your words held value
"I shall kiss you forever"
You were always quite clever
I would have followed you wherever
We danced all night
Our future was clear in my sight
This will last
No need to ever revisit the past
Your eyes saw my soul
A part of me no one has ever known
Young love so intoxicating
I let it swallow me whole
Learning every inch of you
You filled me to my brim
I was taught it was a sin
To feel and touch someone in this way
A young heart obsessed with your soul
How could I know
That nothing lasts forever
When you are just nineteen

Her breasts spoke louder than her words

No matter how thoughtful

No matter how smart

Or educated

Witty Wise

Funny

Insightful

Her voluptuous figure was always louder than the words from her
    lips

She knew and wished he would hear

Wishing she could silence her body

Hide it

Cover it

And be heard

But no matter how hard she tried

All he would and will ever hear

Are the curves of her body

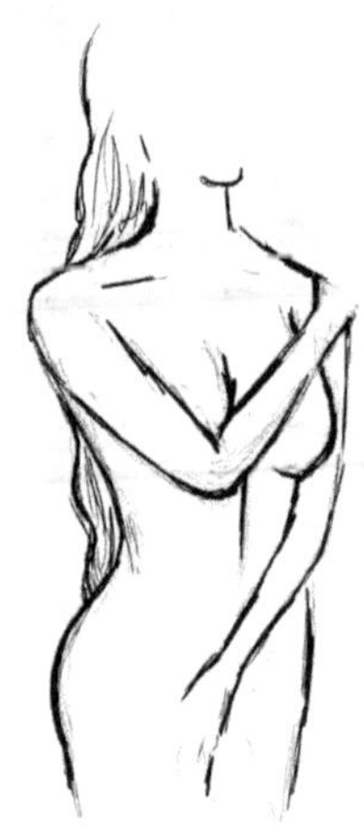

Loud parties gather on a Saturday night

I hear the giggles from flirtatious girls

And rough laughs of men trying hard to impress them

I hear the music turned way too loudly

The bodies moving from side to side

Rhythm is a dime a dozen

I stretch my legs underneath my desk

My pen to the paper as I pour out my heart

Memorizing my lines, creating depth to words on nothing but a
    page

I look around my empty room

My hair greasy from lack of care

Lips chapped from sleepless nights

Body sore from pushing its limits

I press my eyes shut tightly

I imagine being a body in that crowded party

Sweat from warm bodies rubbing on my exposed skin

My tight dress bringing me momentary attention

With no real meaning behind it

The laughs and smiles come mainly from the liquor with no real
    reward

My eyes open, back in my empty room

Loneliness overwhelms me but I do my best to welcome it

She isn't so bad after all

I move my pen slowly back to the paper

Focused on the vision in my head rather than the outside fun of a
    world

too consumed with online presences

Self-doubt consumes my brain as I do mental flips to get around it

Am I delusional?

I consider it, but decide against letting myself know the answer
    just yet
For now, this is my
Saturday night

Warm bodies in a dark room

He brushes his hand across my bare leg

I melt with pleasure from the touch

I can't deny his rough hands feel nice even if no heart stands be-
hind them

Just another man who doesn't know

He doesn't know about the days I cried

So hard I thought I would drown

The way I snort when I laugh too loudly

That my passions consume my thoughts

How I obsess over books and poetry

He doesn't know, nor will he ever

Nor does he care to dive head first into my soul

Does he even know I have one?

The depths of my heart tucked away

I am a body

Warm, sexy, and every inch of me a new curve

For his enjoyment

He has no desire to unlock my heart

So I lay awake

Attempting to accept my place as just a body

My heart skips a beat when I hear his voice
My words suddenly hard to find
I trip over them now unsure if I know how to speak
My high heels now hard to balance in
I am a giraffe new to these legs
As I fumble awkwardly
Uncomfortable laughter fills the silence
How does he do this to me
I crumble under his presence
His rough hand grazes my arm
I hold my breath
Does he notice the racing of my heartbeat?
I collect myself with a smile
Trying to sound cool and charming
I hope to God I am not alarming
I want him to want me the way that
I so desperately want him
His collected composure hard to read
We shouldn't rush this with speed
I want to dive in deep
Does he know?

The world is too loud
Too fast
Too brash
My only comfort from it is in his arms
It's quiet here
I can finally breathe with ease
No tightness lingers in my chest
As I close my eyes knowing this might not last
But for now I enjoy my easy breath
I soak in the silence
His smell the only thing I focus on
No meetings, no work, no chaos
Just him holding me
Protecting me from my own thoughts
I'm unsure if I can trust his words
They are sweet
Too sweet
I've heard them all before
How many more times do I try
Before I give up believing that one might actually
Hold meaning
At least in this moment
It is silent

You are the only one I love
You are the only body I touch
You are everything to me
The younger girl in the tight dress doesn't catch my eye
Or cross my mind
I do not fantasize about sex with her
I do not wish to put my hands on her breasts
I do not wish to wine and dine her
I do not get bored of making love to you
Each time is exciting and new
Loving one woman is enough
The beautiful lies told so easily
I want so badly to believe
That I am enough
How I wish it were true
But every woman knows
Men lie
Women believe
And this is the only way we can all live in harmony

One heart broken too many times to count
Hurt beyond repair
But still going back to give it another try
At this point I am the fool
I am to be blamed
For my own demise
I need to be more wise
Stop going back for more
Love hurts
Why do I want it so badly?
Society sold me a pretty lie wrapped in shiny paper
Only to be unwrapped and discover coal
Hot coal
It burns
I touch it anyways
I cry
I can't touch it again or it will leave a nasty scar
But I push through the pain
I now have many marks on my heart
All nasty scars
Getting rid of them impossible
Once there, they never leave
All I can do is embrace the marks left behind
I do not desire any more scars
I have too many now to count
But I keep touching the coal
It looks so different wrapped in a pretty little box
I can't stop opening it
Hoping for a different result
Attempting again and again
At love

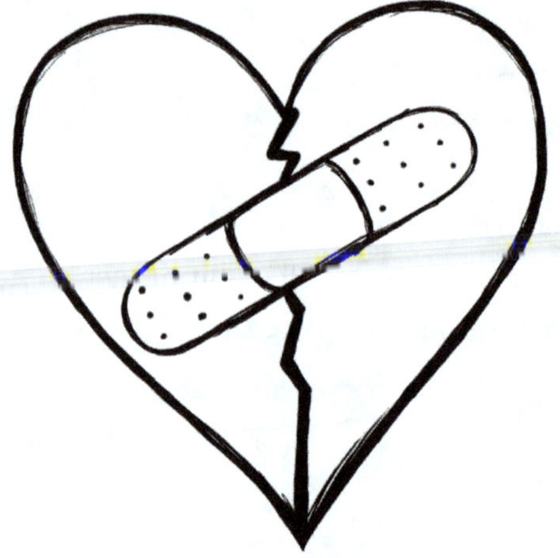

She allows me to run
To dance
To skip down the stairs in the mornings
And curl into bed in the night
She holds me while I cry
While I laugh
Or when I get tripped up on my own two feet
But still I pressure her
I pressure her to be thin
To be tan
To emulate what I see in the magazines
To fit into that tiny dress in the back of my closet
She begs me to just throw it out
I tell her no
She begs me to be accommodating to her ever changing form
She begs me to be kind to her
All she wants is acceptance, nothing more I cannot give it to her
After all she does for me
She only asks for one thing in return
Love
The one thing I cannot give to her

She's tall and effortlessly cool
Men follow her around like puppies
They bring her gifts, all desperate for her attention
The competition for her is steep
I watch with envy
Not one of them notices me
I try to catch the attention of one of the men
He ignores me, his eyes focused on her
I feel invisible
I imagine what it would be like to be her
To have unlimited options
Adoring men bringing me roses
She giggles and does her own thing
Unbothered by the male gaze
While I am desperate to have it
I push my small breasts together
Hoping to catch an eye
They fall flat
I hang my head in defeat
Jealousy is an ugly trait
But often one hard to avoid
I let it linger
She is my friend
I should not have these feelings
But they consume me

No worries in the world

My days consisted of sneaking candy from the pantry

Stealing clothes from my mom's closet

Playing with barbie dolls

Polly pockets

Having sleepovers with my friends

Everything new and exciting

Unlimited possibilities

I could be a princess

A diva

A popstar

An actress

Anything my heart desired

What I would give to be her again

That little girl with a big heart and open mind

Just twelve years old
My body now under constant judgment
"Watch your weight"
"You shouldn't eat that"
Now I hesitate before eating the cookie
Or drinking the milkshake
Calories are terrifying
Can I survive without them?
I'm not sure but I will try
My tummy growls
I ignore it
Hoping my class doesn't hear
I'm on a diet
Just like my mom and her friends
This is what adults do
I'm just fitting in
Carrots are good for you
I watch as my classmates eat delightful baked goods
If I close my eyes tight enough
Maybe my carrot sticks will taste
Like that creamy iced cinnamon roll
In the hands of the boy beside me
He asks if I want a bite
"No, I'm on a diet"
"A what?"
He doesn't know
His body is not under criticism like my own
I sigh, eating another carrot stick

diet

I scurry quickly in the darkness
He invited me out for drinks
8 pm
He walked to the restaurant
Without fear or even a second thought I took an uber
I kept my headphones in, but the driver proceeded to ask too much
And to look too long
I felt uncomfortable
I pulled my tight skirt down to make it seem longer
Closing my jacket to cover my breasts
The date was fun
Enjoyable
He seems like a cool guy
But now, it's over
The night is where I am left
He does not offer to help get me home
Now I am left to navigate this alone with tequila on my breath
My brain thinking slower than usual
I feel the eyes of men watching me as I quickly call a ride
I pray he does not hurt me
I look over my shoulders
Left then right
Hoping no one sneaks up behind me
Fear
Terror
The what if's of a man grabbing me
Shoving me into his car
And never seeing my family or friends again
All for drinks with a man from the internet
Was the fun night worth the risk of this moment?

I just want to get home
Alive

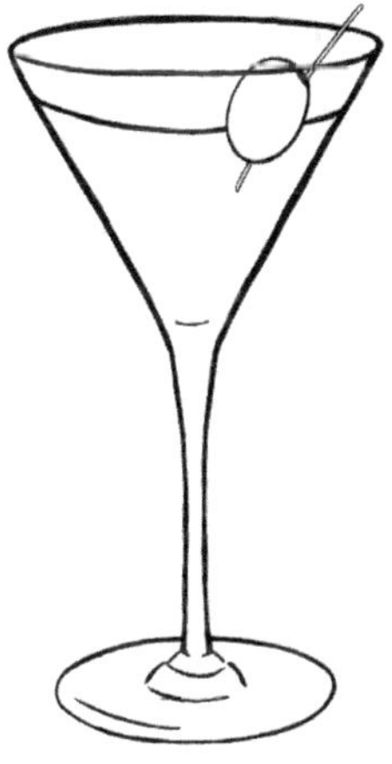

Listen when she speaks
Figure out why she cries
What breaks her
What strengthens her
The things that make her laugh
Your goal being to increase the number of smile lines on her face
Welcome them
Love them
Encourage her to order dessert
Order her an extra glass of wine with dinner
Draw her a hot bath
Play her favorite song in the car
Let her ramble away and do not try to fix it
Just be an ear for her to vent to
Touch her
Gently
Sometimes rough when she wants it
Be her protector and her friend
Her lover
Her partner
Show her she can trust you
A man of your word
What you say you mean
She won't question you
When you earn her respect
No need for nagging
She feels feminine in your presence
Hold her tightly
She will give you her heart
It will be worth keeping

One day happy
The next sad
Moods changing quicker than the minutes in a day
I cannot control
How each external shift affects me
Sometimes it's all internal and even I cannot fix the puzzle
I am a mystery to myself
I cry
I yell
I laugh at the silliness of it all
My moods coming and going like the fall breeze
I allow them to take me where they wish
Embracing everything it means to be a woman

Darling,
You were perfect all along
No makeup or dress
Made you more beautiful
The beauty was always within you

Stop chasing him
You are too lovely to waste a second longer
On a man who cannot see your worth
Choose yourself
Turn your focus inwards
And watch as your life turns into a miracle

He was never who you thought he was
A villain dressed as a sheep
Now you see him
The real him
Accept it and move forward
Not even you can make him become the man
He claimed to be

Outward beauty may catch attention
But darling, your heart is magic
Shining so bright
Winning against the stars
Continue to nurture your soul
In it is where your true beauty lies

You are magic
Your curves
Your smile
Your laugh
Even when it's too loud
Your skin
Even when covered in blemishes
Everything you are
Is unique
No one could ever compete

Complicated yet simple
Loud yet sometimes quiet
Shy yet unusually outgoing
Girl, you do not have to fit into one box
Or one word
You are a rare combination of it all

Be loud
Speak with confidence
Trust your words
Believe in your voice
And in your mind
It has the power to change the world

She was stronger than she knew
No force in the world could stop her
Her energy was magnetic
Everything she wanted
She manifested

He spoke to her gently when he was angry
His voice did not raise
His hands he kept to himself
This was new to her
She expected to feel afraid
But instead, she felt heard
He tried to understand her
Without frightening her
Men like this existed
She just had never had one
Now she did
Tears formed in her eyes
She ran to him
Wanting to be held
She felt safe
For the first time
In the presence of an angry man

She wanted to marry a man like her father
He was protective and kind
Supportive yet firm
Selfless at all times
He would bring a ladder into her room
Just to kill a spider on the ceiling
He never complained
Every word he said he meant
She never doubted him
His words held value to her
But when she dated she could not seem to find him
The men said things they did not mean
And lied without regret
Not one offered to kill the spider on her ceiling
Where were the men like her father?

Be sexy yet naive
Attract men with your clothes
But not too many
Or you are a slut
Let him speak first and agree with what he says
But be vocal enough to hold his attention
Fight back
But not too hard
Or you are a bitch
Be nice
But do not let them run over you
Be smart
But never smarter than him
Make him wait so he respects you
But not too long or he will get bored
The expectations men have set
We try hard to follow
But it was never a war we could win

With age friendships come and go
Usually there is no reason why
People move
Get married
Have children
Get a new job
Everyone is busy
Too busy to laugh with an old friend
The days of stomach curling laughter
Now gone
Just a memory
We had promised to be best friends forever
But that never means much
So I will tuck our good times into the depths of my heart
And lock them in there
So they are there if you ever come back
Only you have the key to unlock them
They may never be opened
And I'm learning to live with that
Old friends traded in for the new
It's just how life goes
May we treasure our time as friends
And maybe in the next life
We will be less busy

Two girls
Similar looking on the outside
Completely different on the inside
But still they connect
On a deeper level
Than any other two girls
Sharing a love
Unbreakable
Every secret kept
Giggles shared
They watch each other
Grow from little girls
Into women
Distance never affecting their bond
Two girls
Called sisters

A best-friend
Hard to find
Most secrets are spilled
Gossip is told
Calls are not returned
Everything feels like a competition
When that's different
And trust is there
She can share the darkest parts of her past
Finally she can breathe
She has someone she can keep
The man who broke her
Doesn't seem so important
When she can call
Her best-friend

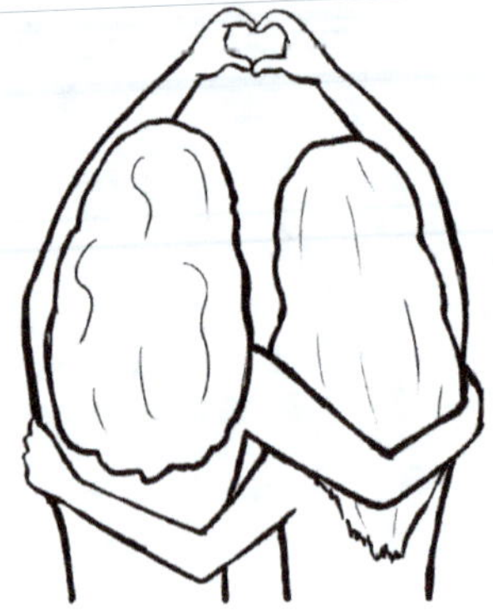

Bathroom floor
My body spread across the tile
It's cold
Goosebumps cover me
Tears flow
They won't stop
I keep quiet
Hoping no one will hear
What happens on the bathroom floor
Must stay behind the door

They age together
No life stage
Separates them
The times they have no money
He is so funny
She forgets the struggles
They endure
His humor captivates her
For years
Then for decades
And sometimes for a lifetime

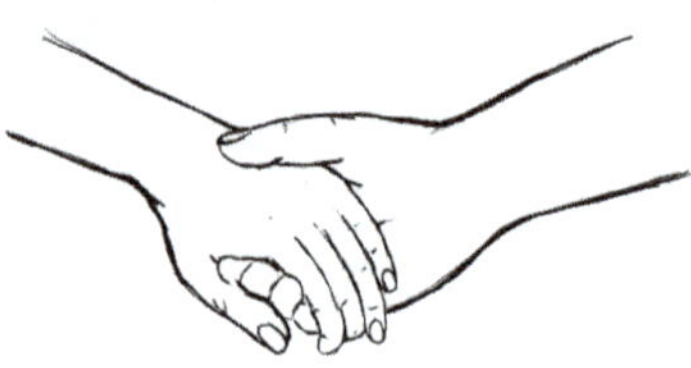

She didn't know what she wanted
Maybe it was
Someone to hold her
To help mold her
Into the women she wanted to be
He wouldn't hold her back
When she wanted to jump
He was there to catch her
If everything went wrong
No matter how many times
He never wanted to dull her
He loved when she shined
She felt no limits in his presence
Maybe love wasn't about anything else
The stories she read
Didn't mean anything if she had to hide away
Shying away from the world
In fear he would be jealous
That felt like prison
A cell she never wanted to enter
No man was worth her freedom
But a love that allowed for dreams
A love that encouraged
A love that supported
He provided something different from the others
This was a love she finally wanted to keep

She will give you everything
Laughter
Wisdom
A place you can share your hearts deepest wounds
She will make you better
Help you achieve
Everything you ever wished for
All she asks is to be cherished
To be loved
Held
And never taken for granted

The sun will rise
Her heart will break
And even though it aches
The sun will set
Each day passing by
Growing closer
To her becoming whole again

She found love
In her best friend's laugh
In her passion for art
In movement through dance
She was fulfilled
Even if she slept alone at night

Missing him
Felt like the ocean
As she stood in the sand
Overlooking it's vastness
Where did it end?

His second choice
Never his first
So close to forever
Yet, so far

The movies made it seem
So simple
Boy meets girl
They decide to give it a whirl
And it works
For eternity
Oh, how she wished reality was just as easy

Loving herself
Became her focus
Knowing her own darkest corner
It wasn't an easy task
What she hid from most

Did anyone care
To hear what she dreamed?
Her deepest desires
Her wildest fantasies
She began to speak
Yet no one listened
Just as she suspected
Not many cared to know
What lived in her
Complicated yet
Beautiful mind

One day
Things would work out
That's what they told her
Her dream job
A loving husband
It would all come together
But, when she looked around
Everyone seemed so sad
Lost in the mundanity of
Their own lives

Was it so bad?
To want more from her life
Adventure and freedom
Yet, stability and love
Could she have it all
Or would she eventually
Have to choose?

She obsessed over pink
Her collection of shoes
Taking up most of her closet
She spent hours perfecting
Her makeup
Her lipliner
She found joy
In pretending she was the barbie
She spent her whole childhood
Idolizing

Another birthday
He forgot
Not even a flower
On the kitchen table
She tried to hold back her tears
How could a man she loved
So deeply
Care so little about her heart?

She thought of ways to
Make him smile
His favorite candy
His favorite color
Tickets to his favorite sports game
Constantly seeking to bring him
Pleasure
But when did he do the same for her?

Nothing lasts
So while it's here
It's best to set it on fire
Burn it in passion
And watch as the flames
Consume it whole

She loved hard and deep
Even if it left
Her broken
She knew her heart would
Be a token
When the right man
Finally found her

Her mood could change quickly
Loving in one moment
Your worst nightmare in the next
From laughter to tears
She was unpredictable
And that's why he did everything
He could to keep her

She moved loudly
Through life
Causing chaos with her
Every move

Her strong opinions
Her desire to never settle
Made her joyful
Yet never content
No one could cage her

She needed adventure
He needed stability
Love would never be
Enough to hold them together
Their memories would have to
Last them both
A lifetime

Her scars
She dressed in perfume
Hid with floral dresses
Masked in a bright smile
Never letting anyone get too close
For fear if they saw the ugly
Underneath her outward beauty
They would toss her away

It seemed so simple
To dive head first into the water
Without fear of crashing at the bottom
With age it did not seem so simple
Everything could hurt
Most things did
Was any of it worth the risk?

My favorite flowers
A song we call ours
Daily texts
Hour long calls
Endless laughter
All of it was fun
Until it ends
The song once ours
I can never play
The flowers you gave
I never buy them again
The heart next to your name
Gone
A contact no longer saved

Meeting you
My first butterflies in forever
I attempt to push them down
Fearing what may come
If I allow them in
Maybe if I delete you
From my memory
My phone
The possibility of hurt is
Rarely worth it

Tell me your favorite color
What movie makes you laugh
Which books make you cry
Every minor detail
That made you the man
I so deeply love

My worth so wrapped up
In others opinions of me
They speak behind my back
Laugh when I act too strange
My mission now to please them
Instead of myself
A miserable way to live

She loved too deeply
Always leaving her hurt
Staying cold
Made her seem bold
Strong
Independent
This was easier than opening
Her heart
Yet again,
To be broken

Purpose
So important
Yet, hard to find
Could she choose just one?
Did purpose have to have one meaning
She never wanted to cage herself
Into choosing just one life to live
She wanted many
Her ever-changing hobbies and interests
The intensity she put into each thing she chose
One purpose would never fulfill her

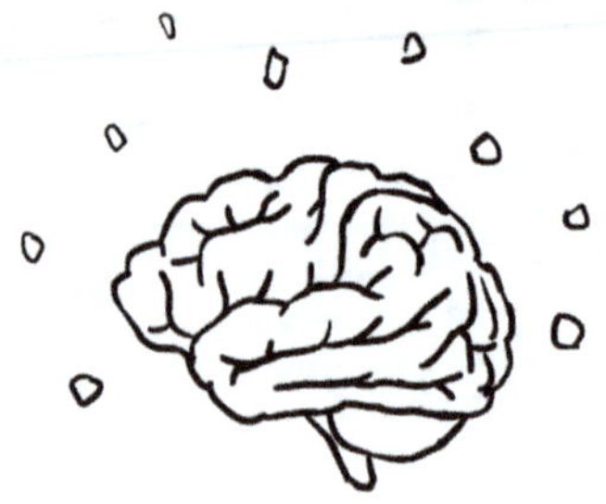

She was wild at times
Quiet at others
Dancing on the tables
Causing a scene
Or in the corner
Reading quietly to herself
She was naive and innocent
Yet could run laps around most mentally
No one word could quite define her
She felt different
Never quite fitting in with any crowd

I want to be alone
But when I am
I wish others were there
To be by myself
Or surrounded in a crowd
Neither ever felt right
What was I looking for in this thing we call life?

One day here
The next there
Never staying long enough
To form something meaningful
Today lovers
Tomorrow strangers
Life on the move was a whirlwind
She could never get her feet on the ground

Her mind he envied
The way other men looked at her
Made him rage in anger
He blamed her
For her beauty
Her clothes
The way she lit up a room
She tried to dull herself
To please him
But truth is, he hated her
His jealousy ate at him
He would never love her
The way she wanted to be loved

All her life
She chased the feeling he gave her
The passion and fire
The type of thing that comes only once
It would never be replicated
She knew it
But still, she looked for him in everyone she met
Holding hope that one day she might find
A glimpse of what he was to her

Happiness flowed in waves
Hitting highs
Then suddenly falling flat
The ups and downs
Hard to navigate
With no way to predict if a high was coming
Or an ultimate low

She wanted to call him
To say everything on her heart
To spill her feelings as quickly as water running from a faucet
Always too fast but straight to the point
Instead, she stopped herself
She didn't want to know if he cared to hear
What she felt
It was better to cut him off and let things die before they really began